"This book may convert 20,000,000 Democrats."

James T. Kelly

This book has been creatively configured for optimum presentation on Amazon.com.

This American copy was printed in the United States of America. Amazon may print in Europe and Asia to fill orders in those local markets.

The font is Franklin Gothic Medium out of my great admiration and respect for Benjamin Franklin.

I alone am solely responsible for the contents of this book.

Order additional copies from www.createspace.com/4251749

Originally published September 20, 2013
Release VIII - April 20, 2016

Thank you for picking up this little book.

You are about to learn some little known history of which president set our nation on our six decades downhill course.

You will learn about when America was the greatest manufacturing nation in history, and which political party seems to be bent on destroying it.

You will learn how TAX THE RICH policies doubled, then redoubled, then tripled, then quadrupled the cost of a 'starter' home. It sold new in 1947 for $7,990, but now costs $380,000 as a fixer upper.

High taxes are killing our nation by killing family formation.

You will learn how your children and grandchildren may be forced to pay up to $325 interest (instead of only $32 interest) on each $100 of their home mortgage.

That translates into $493,749.39 of interest alone on a modest $150,000 - 30 year home mortgage.

You will read of what causes all the inflation that is destroying the buying power of your savings, your life insurance, your pension and your Social Security.

You will learn how certain laws are destroying our cities and impoverishing about one third of our population.

You will learn why "high tax rates" are not the correct way to "tax the rich." Instead, they drive our National Debt higher.

You will learn how lower tax rates and limiting certain tax deductions will reverse 65 years of damage.

And you can learn all of this in about one hour.

James T. Kelly

Dedication:

This work is dedicated to Ginny, my wonderful wife of 64 years, and also to our children and many grandchildren.

First she filled my life with the joys of dating.

Next she filled my heart with the joys of marriage.

Then we shared a joyful struggle of raising children.

Now we enjoy our Grandchildren, and pray we will see some great-grandchildren in this brief span called our lifetime.

She has had the courage to endure my taking risks as I have stumbled through life in one endless sequence of adventuress learning experiences.

Her courage to emulate the life of Saint Theresa, the Little Flower, gave me the courage to live my life like Don Quixote, The Man of LaMancha, pursuing and accomplishing a few Impossible Dreams.

The Windmill I am targeting in this work is the currently flawed Internal Revenue Code that was created by the Ghosts of Congress past.

The present generation must work to produce a Smart Tax Code so that America may prosper for many generations to come.

Join us in this noble pursuit of making a better America and a better world for all.

As for my Ginny, I think she is practically a Saint already. I thank God for her every day of my life.

Jim Kelly

Foreword:

"TAX THE RICH" policies of the Democratic party have done more damage to American families since the 1950's Korean War than all of our wartime enemies have done to us since the 1776 Revolutionary War!

Few Americans know that when President Truman imposed a 52% Corporate Income tax on business, he also raised the top individual tax rate from 91% to 92%. The owners of the factories that won WWII only kept four cents of the last dollar they earned.

High tax rates increased tax shelter borrowing. Excessive borrowing caused high interest rates High interest rates made home mortgages more expensive. High taxes spurred job outsourcing. Lost jobs increased unemployment. Unemployment lowered living standards. Jobless people raised welfare costs. High interest rates added 10 years to mortgages. Every one of the above increased our national debt.

Tax laws went counterproductive after high tax rates made massive borrowing profitable to the rich. That created a "Debt Preference" tax code. Voters supporting "TAX THE RICH" politicians end up paying dearly for their misguided prejudice.

My proposed "Equity Preference" or "Smart" Tax Code could lift millions out of poverty and restore the greatness of America.

My talent is limited. However I sold Federal and State Tax and business Law reports, plus computer tax return service for 20 years. That gave me access to tax facts few tax professionals, including members of Congress, are aware of. Also, my early inventor training in a Union Carbide laboratory included "Question everything."

The Kennedy family, a Rockefeller family, Fortune 500 firms, major banks, Wall Street brokers and lawyers, and scores of accounting and law firms, some serving Rock Stars and Movie Stars, were my former customers.

James T. Kelly
Middle Class Tax Advocate
and Grandfather of many.

PREFACE:

These events laid the foundation for some of our current problems.

May 8, 1945 - Germany surrendered, ending World War II in Europe. German factories had been reduced to rubble. Few buildings taller than two floors were left standing.

April 12, 1945 - President Franklin Delano Roosevelt died in office. Vice President Harry S. Truman became the 33rd President.

August 14, 1945 - Japan surrendered to General Douglas MacArthur, ending World War II in Asia. MacArthur wired Truman,"Send bullets or food." We sent food.

Observation: There were no German, Italian or Japanese imports into America during World War II. We manufactured all we needed.

At the end of WWII in 1945 the United States was the greatest manufacturing nation in the history of the world. American firms that won the 'factory output' war converted to peacetime production.

June 5, 1947 - U.S. Secretary of State George C. Marshall proposed a plan to help rebuild Europe, combining financial aid with relaxed trade barriers.

Nov. 2, 1948 - Harry S. Truman elected President. The Democratic Party retook both the Senate and the House of Representatives.

June 25, 1950 - North Korea invaded South Korea.

June 30, 1950 - America had not been attacked nor did North Korea declare war on the United States. Still, President Truman ordered American ground forces into Korea. War hero General Douglas MacArthur commanded the U.S. (and United Nations) troops.

Soon afterward, Truman increased the corporate tax rate to 52% and the personal tax rate to 92%. -i.e. GREED BEGAN in the WHITE HOUSE.

Truman put 300,000 U.S. Troops into the Korean conflict. U.S. Dead: 36,579. N. & S. Korea and China, dead or missing: 2,860,000.

Observation: America has protected South Korea, at our expense, for 66 years and counting as of 2016. Why are we paying their bills?

GREED BEGAN IN THE WHITE HOUSE

Following his 2015 State of the Union address, I wrote to President Obama,

I don't want to hurt your feelings, but "TAX THE RICH" policies of the Democratic Party have done more damage to American families since the 1950 Korean War than all of our wartime enemies have done to us since the 1776 Revolutionary War!

At age 53, you are simply too young to have experienced the damage done by President Truman's "TAX THE RICH" policy.

Before you were born, I helped: 1) get the first rockets off of Cape Canaveral; 2) get the first jet engines certified for commercial airlines; 3) build the first liquid oxygen system for space flights; and 4) automate the manufacture of industrial gas cylinders. In 1958 the Speedway, Indiana, facility was shipped out and I went unemployed. The cause: "TAX THE RICH" policy of President Truman.

Homeowners at 24/22, we lost everything. By 1966 my family of seven were living in a 700 square foot rented NY apartment. No job. No car. No insurance. By 1968 my wife was down to just three cents and half a bottle of catchup at what shaped up as our personal Last Supper. Details are in one of my two other books listed at the PS below.

Enclosed is a copy of my newest self-published book,

GREED BEGAN IN THE WHITE HOUSE
A discovery inspired by Albert Einstein

It shows that "TAX THE RICH" policies of your party are 180 degrees off course. I propose replacing the current 'Debt Preference' tax code with an 'Equity Preference' tax code.

Respectfully,

James T. Kelly
Middle Class Tax Advocate
And Grandfather of many

PS. The book of our 60 years of marriage can be previewed at www.LoveAdventureHappiness.com. That web site has book reviews and a link to another book, Where Does Music Come From? Your girls might enjoy singing one or more of my 19 original songs.

GREED
BEGAN
IN
THE
WHITE HOUSE

Chapter 1

"The hardest thing to understand in the world is the income tax."
Albert Einstein, 1879-1955

He made this comment to Leo Mattersdorf, who prepared his tax returns from his arrival in America in 1933 until his death.

This quotation excuses many current and former elected officials. If Einstein could not understand it, we should not expect the ordinary humans in government to understand our income tax laws either.

During the Korean War, Democratic President Truman raised the corporate tax rate from 42% to 52% and the top personal income tax rate from 91% to 92%. His was the most destructive tax law in history. Truman's high tax rates launched the dismantling of American manufacturing. They also cost Baby Boomers billions in excess mortgage expense. Even the Baby Boomer's grandchildren are still paying for Truman's actions.

President Reagan cut the top corporate tax to 27%.
President Obama raised it back to 39%.
An Equity Preference tax code might top out at about 24%.

High tax rates are driving 'outsourcing,' killing American jobs, forcing people onto welfare and increasing our tax burdens by cutting tax revenue from domestic manufacturing. "TAX THE RICH" policies have been a Lose-Lose-Lose for much of the world.

How high were the historic corporate income tax rates?

1913	Pre WW I	1 percent
1920	Post WW I	10 percent
1930	Depression	12 percent
1940	Pre WW II	38 percent
1950	Post WW II	42 percent

After North Korea invaded South Korea. President Truman Raised the corporate income tax rate still higher.

1952	52 percent

End of chapter

Chapter 2

HOW HIGH WERE PERSONAL TAX RATES?

Few people on Earth know that when President Truman started taking 52% of corporations profits, he was also taking up to 92% of the personal income of some owners.

The business owners that built our ships, tanks, planes, guns and bombs that won WWII were severely punished for helping America defeat Germany, Italy and Japan. Democratic President Truman's high tax rates confiscated all but a four cents on a dollar of their earnings.

What motivated President Truman to put crippling taxes on the very people that made America great and strong?

A brief review of his life before entering politics tells the story. Born in 1884 to a farm family, he had several career options. After serving successfully in the U. S. Army during World War I, he and a partner opened a haberdashery shop in 1919 at age 35.

Three years later, in 1922, he was forced to close his doors at age 38, leaving him deeply in debt. That was seven years before the start of the Great Depression.

A failure in his first chosen profession, one might assume he had little affection for banks and bankers whose rules and policies may have helped to force him out of business.

Or was it just plain and simple ENVY and JEALOUSY!

End of chapter

Chapter 3

How did Wall Street respond to Truman's tax rates?

They used the tax code to 'break even' or 'get even.'

On November 29, 1951 the New York Times reported that Union Carbide and Westinghouse Electric borrowed $550,000,000 from Met Life and Prudential for a term of 100 years at 3 ½ and 3 ¾% interest. (I was then serving in the U.S. army during the Korean War.)

The 3 1/2% interest rate sounds cheap by standards since 1960. But I dug deeper.

About ten years earlier, on Dec. 4, 1941, in the week before Pearl Harbor, the Treasury borrowed $1,000,000,000 (one billion) of new money for 25 and 30 year bonds.

Those 1967-1972 maturities paid 2 1/2% interest. Also that day Treasury borrowed $500,000,000 (half a billion) in 10 & 15 years bonds paying 2%.

After the Met Life and Prudential loans, the U. S. Government had to equal or surpass the 3 1/2% interest.

Those 100 year loans were paid off in 25 years, but the higher interest rates remained for decades.

The Federal Reserve Board Chairman Paul Volker pushed some rates over 15% during the Reagan administration. (1981-1989)

That proves that President Truman's "TAX THE RICH" policy raised borrowing costs for every level of government, every business, every family and every college student since 1952!

End of chapter

Chapter 4

Why Wall Street responded

Why did two giant enterprises suddenly take on massive debt?

To recover the profits that Truman had taxed away!

Follow the brilliant logic that has been largely hidden from public view since 1952.

A hypothetical company earned $1,000,000 before taxes.
It was a 6% return on investment.
They had a net worth of $16,666,666, with zero debt.
Then the Truman Tax took $520,000 off the top.
The company had $480,000 profit after taxes.
That was only 2.88% return on investment.
The company borrowed $16,666,666 at 4% interest.
They then had twice as much cash to invest, and again earned 6% on the money.
They then had $2,000,000 in profit before taxes and interest.
The interest cost was 4% of $1 million, or $400,000.
Interest was tax deductible; so taxable income was $1,600,000 They paid 52% in taxes, or $832,000, leaving them with {$1,600,000 minus $832,000} for a net profit of $768,000.

With $768,000 net profit after interest and taxes, the business realized a 7.68% return on investment.

That was far better than the 2.88% Truman had left them.

This is an illustration, not an actual case, of the interactive nature of the tax code of the United States. It explains the motive for two giant loans by large established successful enterprises.

End of chapter

Chapter 5

What really happened?

The business owners that built our ships, tanks, planes, guns and bombs that won WWII were not a bunch of dummies.

They were the DuPont's, Rockefeller's, Ford's, Firestone's, Edison's, Melon's, Grace's, Kaiser's, Grumman's and many other families behind our chemical, oil, automotive, electrical, banking, railroads, steel, tires, utilities, ship building and aircraft manufacturing industries.

Here is just one example of their brilliance.

It normally took a year or more to build a ship. But Henry J. Kaiser had learned from Henry Ford's assembly line. He laid the keel for the 10,500 ton Robert E. Peary on Sunday, November 8, 1942, and launched it 4 days and 15 ½ hours later.

Despite his great skills, Mr. Kaiser was one of the lesser stars of American industry.

Those brilliant and successful industrialists saw clearly that Truman targeted them out of envy and jealousy.

They found a solution.

They used the tax code against Truman.

End of chapter

Chapter 6

WHAT ELSE HAPPENED?

When President Truman raised tax rates, smarter people outsmarted him.

Truman and his advisors failed to understand the interactive nature of tax math.

When Truman took 52% of the corporate profits in taxes, corporations borrowed for tax advantage.

The interest they paid to banks and insurance companies, and to the public, generated huge tax deductions.

In other words, the government was paying 52% of the cost of the massive corporate borrowing.

The government was also paying for much of the 92% tax rate on wealthy people who also borrowed heavily over the decades via Tax Shelters.

Since "We the People" are the ultimate government, Democrat Harry S. Truman's "TAX THE RICH" policy piled his high tax and debt burdens on the American people.

In plain English, Democratic President Harry S. Truman's high tax rates shot America in the foot, knee, heart and pocketbook.

Those wounds have not yet healed, which is why America and her working families are still bleeding money.

End of chapter

Chapter 7

PRESIDENT TRUMAN'S FIRST GREAT MISTAKE

Prior to his raising tax rates to 52% and 92%, borrowing had been costly to borrowers since the days of Cleopatra.

With Truman's high tax rates, borrowing became profitable to high income taxpayers. That set inflation on fire.

How big is the problem?

When Union Carbide and Westinghouse borrowed the $550,000,000, a typical mortgage was well under $10,000.

Those two massive loans crowded out home mortgages for over 5,500 families, pricing many out of home ownership forever.

The U.S. Treasury borrowing cost, only 2% before Pearl Harbor, soon doubled, redoubled, redoubled again, then rose still higher.

Hirer interest rates piled budget troubles upon every president, governor, mayor, city manager, school board, business and family since Democratic President Harry Truman imposed his "TAX THE RICH" confiscatory tax rates.

The inflation caused by high tax rates has been nonstop for over half a century with no sign of stopping.

What is the average home mortgage today?

What is YOUR home mortgage?

What will your children's mortgages cost them?
(Look for examples later in this book.)

End of chapter

Chapter 8

The CPI reflects inflation

The U.S. Bureau of Labor Statistics tracks the cost of all the things all Americans buy. They publish the results in the form of the Consumer Price Index, or CPI. (Now in use 100 years.)

President Reagan (1981-1989) did not like the high value, and directed the Bureau to reset it with a base of 100.

They revalued every year to meet the new base. The graph below reflects the relative value of the CPI for the entire century, 1912 - 2012.

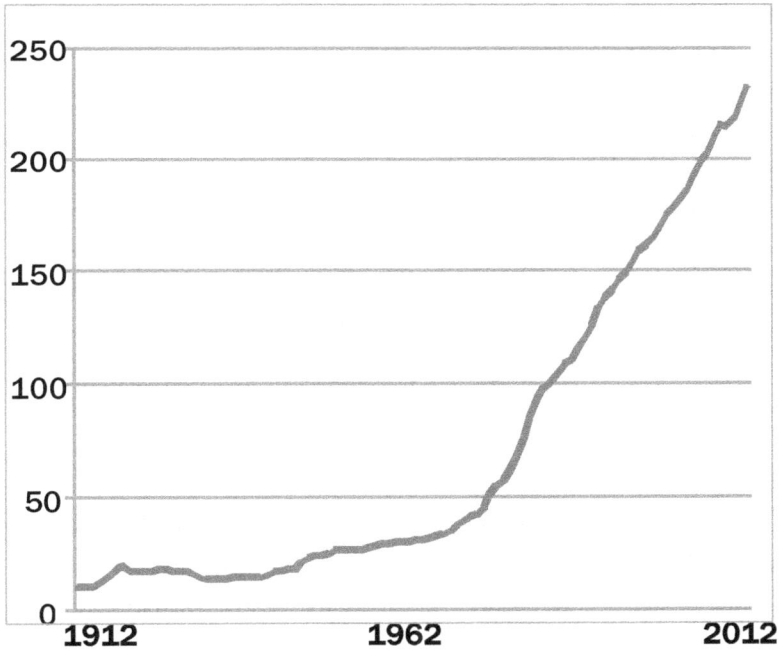

In the decades after Truman, many investors sought high leverage. Junk Bonds became a way for some corporations to pay all of a businesses earnings directly to banks, with Zero taxes.

The money supply grew and inflation soared.

End of chapter

Chapter 9

DID HIGH TAX RATES REDUCE THE NATIONAL DEBT?

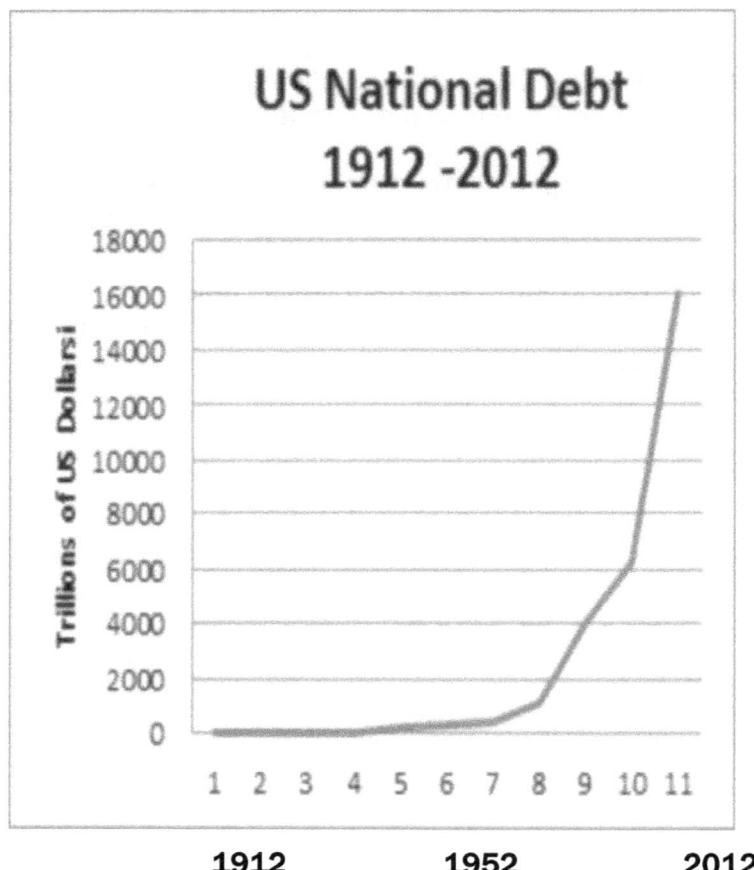

The evidence on this page is very clear. High tax rates failed to cover day to day operating expenses. In fact, higher tax rates have contributed to a greater national debt by increasing the value of tax deductions. This and prior graph are both for 1912-2012.)

That puts Democratic President Truman and all "TAX THE RICH" Democrats in the economic doghouse in so far as their thinking that high tax rates would be beneficial to America.

End of chapter

Chapter

DID HIGH TAX RATES AID AMERICAN BUSINESS?
America's Balance of Trade 1983 - 2012

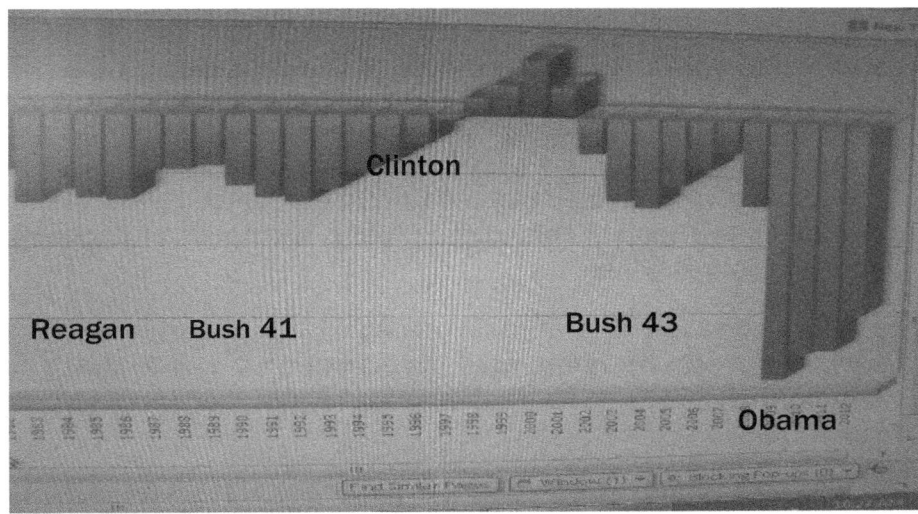

www.davemanuel.com/charts2/surpluses_and_deficits_1940 2011.html (The author photographed above Web page with his Kodak)

==

The above picture clearly shows that the most massive increase in our trade deficit occurred on President Obama's watch in 2009-2012.

Part of this increase may stem from Obama's Cash for Clunkers program. It brought more imported cars into America with little effect on American unemployment of tax revenue. He also hiked welfare cost.

The last brief period of trade surplus (shown as "up") was during the Clinton presidency. Both Presidents Bush ran wartime deficits, as did Presidents Roosevelt, Truman, Kennedy, Johnson and Obama.

The Government Accountability Office, GAO, Spring 2012 report stated "Federal spending will drive the national debt to "unsustainable" levels in the coming decades."

We cannot blame senior citizens for their "earned" benefits. It is "unearned" benefits and giveaways that must be cut.

End of chapter

Chapter 11

ARE HIGH TAX RATES GOOD FOR THE WORLD?

When a Boy Scout or Girl Scout ventured into the woods they carried a compass to help them find their way. Ships on the ocean and all aircraft rely on some form of navigation equipment to guide them safely on their journeys.

Nations and industries use a different kind of compass that they call Economic Theory. I coined the phrase "Compass of Economics" to define tools they use.

Many economists embrace the economic theories of George Maynard Keynes. He formulated his economic theory in the 1930's when borrowing was costly to the borrower. (He died in 1946 before Truman raised taxes.)

When Truman's 1952 high tax rates made massive borrowing profitable to the wealthy, Keynesian Economic Theory was dealt a fatal blow, but nobody noticed.

President Obama's Federal Reserve Chairman Ben Bernanke tried using Keynesian theory to stimulate the U.S. Economy in 2012. He only spurred inflation as reflected in the price of Gold.

In 1971 Gold was officially valued at $35 Dollars per ounce. Two weeks before the 2012 elections, gold was over $1,700 per ounce. From $35 to $1,700 is a lot of inflation in just the few years from President Nixon to President Obama.

A few people made big gains on gold. Most Americans simply lost buying power as inflation stole the value of their paychecks, savings, pensions, life insurance and their hard earned Social Security.

How many nations suffer from American high tax rates and the inflation that they caused in the past and are still causing?

An Equity Preference tax code could stop inflation and save our nation.

End of chapter

Chapter 12

HOW GOVERNMENT HURT FAMILIES

Following WWII 16,000,000 Americans came home from wars around the world. The Government had passed the GI Bill to provide low cost mortgage loans to veterans.

Many married couples wanted to start families, but they could not find suitable housing. Many lived with parents (as my Navy Vet brother did) and more lived in barns, cars, trucks and tool sheds.

JFK and LaGuardia airports are in Queens County. My late father officially took part in buying the land for both airports on behalf of New York City. In neighboring Nassau County, Levittown opened.

By 1949 ex-GI's could buy unattached homes for $7,990. The down payment was $90 and the monthly mortgage payment was $58. They got busy and launched the Baby Boom!

In 1952 my young Brooklyn-born bride and I lived in a converted chicken coop near my Midwestern army base.

In 1953, fresh from my Korean War army service, I rejoined a 230,000-employee Dow Jones company, Union Carbide. My salary Was $295 *per month* as a cost estimator. Soon afterward I was promoted to "Hired inventor."

We bought a brand new small home near Speedway, Indiana, for $9,995, with $2,500 down. The mortgage was $53.71 per month for principle and interest.

The adjusted cost of living index in 1953 was 26.9, but in 2013, at 230.4, it was 857% higher due to inflation caused by the Internal Revenue Code and excessive socialist welfare spending.

Working Middle Class families are falling behind daily.

End of chapter

Chapter 13

HOW FAMILIES WERE HURT

On Wall Street, far from our 24' X 36' one story house without a basement or stand up attic, the ripple effect of Truman's high tax rates began changing the economy for the worse.

A few years after Truman imposed his confiscatory tax rates, prices started rising. In many communities, homes identical to those that once sold for $7,990 were selling for over $15,000.

Banks wanted 10% down, and 8.5%, so the young couples faced mortgages of $13,500 with monthly payments of $117. That was more than double what payments were only a few years earlier.

Extending the mortgage from 20 to 25 years only cut the monthly payment from $117 down to $108.71.

Still out of reach of many families in the 1960's.

In desperation, many opted for 30 year mortgages, and sacrificed to pay $103.80 per month for principle and interest only.
Taxes and insurance were extra.

Many 1970 families were priced out of home ownership and into perpetual renter status, or onto public assistance.

Some of those $7,990 homes are now selling over $300,000.

That is causing great pain to another generation of young families trying to get a toehold on the American Dream.

Tax policy to aid family formation should be the highest priority for national survival.

End of chapter

Chapter 14

IMPACT OF TRUMAN'S FIRST GREAT MISTAKE

This point is worth repeating. Prior to Truman raising tax rates to 52% and 92%, borrowing had been costly to borrowers since the days of Cleopatra.

With Truman's high tax rates, massive borrowing became profitable to high income taxpayers.

When Union Carbide and Westinghouse Electric borrowed $550,000,000 a typical home mortgage was well under $10,000.

Those two massive loans crowded out home mortgages for over 5,500 families, pricing them out of home ownership.

The U.S. Treasury borrowing cost, only 2% before Pearl Harbor, soon rose to 4%, then 8% and then 14%.

Hirer interest rates piled trouble upon every President, Governor, Mayor, City Manager, school board, business and working family since President Harry Truman imposed his confiscatory tax rates.

Every President, Treasury Secretary and Federal Reserve Bank Official, large and small businesses, has felt the painful impact that Truman's confiscatory tax rates started.

Working Middle Class families have carried the brunt of the burdens via high interest rates and extra years of mortgage payments.

Many college students must carry heavy debt, then suffer the lower living standards that debt inflicts upon them for decades to come.

Democrats "TAX THE RICH" policy, with high tax rates, are the worst enemy of every working family on this planet.

End of chapter

Chapter 15

THE MARY AND JOE IMPACT

Wealthy borrowers quickly learned they could be more profitable by taking on heavy debt burdens. They borrowed huge sums from banks. That increased the nations money supply.

Professor Milton Friedman, University of Chicago, was an economic advisor to President Ronald Reagan, (1981 to 1989.)

Dr. Friedman won the Noble Prize in Economics for showing that increasing the money supply contributed to rising prices and inflation.

Across America, families had no option except to pay higher and higher prices for everything they needed.

Did Truman's high tax rates impact home buyers Mary & Joe?

The following example was created to illustrate the impact of Truman's high tax rates on families decades after Truman died.

It is based on $100,000 mortgages with approximately equal monthly payments, but with different interest rates and years of payments.

Family A:

The 4.25% rate was selected to replicate the GI loans of the 1946-1950 era. Family 'A' took a $100,000, 15 year mortgage. The monthly payment for principle and interest was $752.88

Family B:

A few decades later interest rates had more than doubled. In the 1980-1999 (and perhaps later). Family 'B' was forced into a 30 year mortgage to make payments affordable at $769.53.

End of chapter

Chapter 16

THE PAIN HIT FAMILIES

The impact of Truman's high tax rate is best understood by how it hit middle class working families.

COST OF $100,000 HOME MORTGAGE

Family	"A" "	B"
Interest Rate	4.25%	8.50%
Monthly payment	$752.88	$769.53
Term	15 years	30 years
Months	180	360
Total payments	$135,518	$277,031
Interest cost	$35,518	$177,031
Interest as % of mortgage	35.5%	177.0%

The difference in cost is: (277,031-135,518=$141,513)

Many marry by their 30's, then buy homes. Truman's high tax rates put millions of families into mortgage bondage almost for life.

Low interest rates would allow families to be mortgage free 15 years sooner. The $141,513 savings would allow many parents to pay for their children's higher educations without debt burdens or government aid. Or it could help fund their retirement.

Most families pay more money for mortgage interest than they are able to save for their own retirement. Voters should force a change to benefit working families "Married with children."

End of chapter

Chapter 17

GAINING PERSPECTIVE

Most people have heard the phrase, "rate of inflation." We all see it in rising prices on almost every trip to buy anything.

The U.S. Department of Labor Statistics created the Consumer Price Index, or CPI, in 1912, over 100 years ago.

When President Reagan took office, he did not like the then current number, so he directed that they start over. The statisticians computed a new base of 100.

Using that base, they recomputed all earlier years numbers to reflect relative values accurately.

Here are the numbers for 1913 to 1953, the 40 years before the Truman tax rates influenced the results.

1913	10.1
1923	17.3
1933	13.2
1943	17.4
1953	26.9

The rise in prices from 1913 to 1923 were caused in part by World War I, 1914-1919.

The rise in prices from 1943 to 1953 were caused in part by World War II, 1939-1945.

The rise in prices in 1953 were caused in part by Truman's Korean War.

Of course, the rise in prices in 1953 were caused in part by Truman's Korean War.

End of chapter

Chapter 18

SECTION 8 HOUSING

Housing at taxpayer expense began when America was in the middle of the Great Depression. The Roosevelt Administration passed The Housing Act of 1937, which is best known as Section 8 housing.

For over 75 years the number of people living on the taxes paid by others has been growing non-stop.

Truman's high tax rates and high interest rates have been a factor in forcing people into living in the often despised 'projects'.

In many cities, the cost of public housing is a heavy drain on city budgets. Sometimes essential services for schools, police and firefighters have been curtailed.

Detroit, once the shining symbol of American prowess, is broke. That city's collapse is due in part to supporting families that should have been supporting themselves.

Many of those families were forced into public housing after being priced out of private housing by Truman's high tax rates and resulting decades of high interest rates.

These issues beg the question, "Isn't there a better way?"

Early settlers had one road to better living: WORK!
Government created a second path, PUBLIC ASSISTANCE!

Illegal immigrants in the USA get more free benefits than elderly native born World War II Vets who still work and/or pay taxes.

Illegal immigrants in North Korea get six years at hard labor. Can we find a happy and humane middle ground?

Will the leaders for true social justice please run for office?

End of chapter

Chapter 19

INFLATION REVISITED

In 1942, at age 13, I used my little red wagon on the streets of New York City to collect scrap metal for World War II.

A Boy Scout, I was also trained as a Junior Air Raid Warden. In the periodic air raid drills of the time I was required to knock on the door on any house showing lights.

One person I met chatted with me from time to time. He also explained "Wartime inflation" about as follows:

"In normal times, when business or governments spend big money, they get things that they expect to use for many years. A factory, or machinery, or railroad cars and trucks to deliver goods on a lasting basis.

"People used their wages to buy food, clothing and housing."

"In wartime, governments spent much more money to produce the weapons of war. The people are paid even more money due to full employment, but they do not produce products for people to buy.

"People had lots of money, but little to buy, so prices went up."

I never heard economists call it "Wartime inflation" but I saw it happen in my own life.

End of chapter

Chapter 20

PEACETIME INFLATION

His truth: "The government spent much more money but did not produce products that people could buy."

That nugget of truth contains the alternate explanation of the root cause of inflation that both the Noble Prize winner and Noble Prize Committee overlooked. Let me rephrase it.

"Inflation results when government gives money to people who produce nothing durable for society in exchange."

That is a big net. It takes in subsidies paid to farmers for not producing food, plus food stamps and every form of welfare known in America. It also takes in all the foreign aid money spent since the end of World War II.

<u>Congress created these problems. A new Congress must fix them.</u>

Captain John Smith established the first English settlement in North America in 1607. It was up river some 40 miles inland of the ocean, at Jamestown, now part of Virginia.

He ordered: "Those that will not work will not eat."

After further exploration, Captain Smith gave the name "New England" to that region and noted: "Here every man may be master and owner of his owne labour and land... If he have nothing but his hands, he may...by industrie quickly grow rich."

If America is to survive, Democrats and Republicans must go back to Captain John Smith's rule. They need to compromise on laws that require all able bodied citizens to work, and also enable every citizen to 'profit the work of their hands.'

An Equity Preference Tax code will help make that happen.

End of chapter

Chapter 21

TRUMAN'S SECOND GREAT MISTAKE

Raising tax rates was only one of Truman's three great mistakes. His second mistake was his failure to level the playing the field between families and powerful industries.

I write as an eyewitness.

Partnerships, notably real estate syndicates, were exempt from the double taxation imposed on American industrial corporations.

The tragic result has been that the tax advantages of insurance companies and real estate partnerships made it easier for them to buy 1,000 apartments than it was for the average Mary's and Joe's of America to buy a single home. Ditto small business work space.

One such syndicate was controlled by the late Leona Helmsley. She is remembered as a tax-evading millionaire who served time in prison and also as a woman who disinherited her own children but left $11,000,000 to her dog.

Her Helmsley-Spear organization was but one of my many customers. They owned the Empire State Building and other properties in New York and elsewhere. Investments in buildings were allowed to be written off over 50 years. Many buildings over 50 are still taking tax write-offs by selling a building from one owner to another. I define that as 'Serial Repetitive Depreciation." You might also call it "Double Dipping."

This tax loophole may be bigger than the Empire State Building. It could be closed by adding a single sentence to the tax code. "Second and subsequent owners of depreciable assets may only use the unused depreciation of all prior owners regardless of their purchase price."

Closing this giant tax loophole will arrest the decay of cities, reduce the National Debt and aid family formation.

End of chapter

Chapter 22

TRUMAN'S THIRD GREAT MISTAKE

President Truman appointed five star General Douglas MacArthur as post-war head of Japan. MacArthur was one of only five men in history to achieve that exalted rank.

MacArthur refused to allow American-made cars into Japan. He also banned US companies from building factories there.

THE CONSEQUENCES OF TRUMAN'S THIRD GREAT MISTAKE

It was President Truman's lack of oversight that allowed foreign auto makers from Europe and Asia to sell their cars in America. American workers pay American taxes that support our Social Security and our total infrastructure from highways to schools to hospitals and universities. Those taxes also pay for our national defense.

Workers building cars in Europe and Asia do not pay payroll taxes in America to support any of our needs.

Furthermore, the taxes of American workers are paying for the defense of Europe, Japan, Korea and other nations that sell their products in America. American workers subsidize foreign firms that shut American factories and put Americans out of work.

Foreign auto makers have become so powerful that some American firms have gone out of business. Others have teetered on the edge of collapse.

Should imports pay taxes equal to what Americans pay? Should we start charging other nations for the cost of our armed forces defending them? Should we be importing cars when we have unemployment in Detroit?

Why does Congress take from working Middle Class taxpayers and give other people their endless FREE LUNCH?

End of chapter

Chapter 23

WHAT IS TAX FREEDOM DAY?

Tax Freedom Day is the day when the nation as a whole has earned enough money to pay its total tax bill for the year. In 2013, Americans will pay $2.76 trillion in federal taxes and $1.45 trillion in state taxes, for a total tax bill of $4.22 trillion, or 29.4 percent of income. April 18 is 29.4 percent, or 108 days, into the year.

Why is Tax Freedom Day later this year?
Tax Freedom Day is five days later than last year, due mainly to the fiscal cliff deal that raised federal taxes on individual income and payroll. Additionally, the Affordable Care Act's investment tax and excise tax went into effect. Finally, despite these tax increases, the economy is expected to continue its slow recovery, boosting profits, incomes, and tax revenues.

When is Tax Freedom Day if you include federal borrowing?
Since 2002, federal expenses have exceeded federal revenues, with the budget deficit exceeding $1 trillion annually from 2009 to 2012. In 2013, the deficit will come down slightly to $833 billion. If we include this annual federal borrowing, which represents future taxes owed, Tax Freedom Day would occur on May 9, 21 days later. The latest ever deficit-inclusive Tax Freedom Day occurred during World War II, on May 21, 1945.

Founded in 1937, the Tax Foundation is the nation's leading independent, non-partisan organization providing sound research and analysis on federal and state tax policy. The Tax Foundation is a 501(c)(3) non-profit and our offices are located in the National Press Building in Washington, DC.

All information in this chapter came from one source:
http://taxfoundation.org/

End of chapter

Chapter 24

FREE TRADE OR FAIR TRADE?

During the American Revolution in 1775-1783, we had no trade with Great Britain. After Britain recognized us as an independent nation, they sought "Free Trade." Their goal was simple: provide low cost products that would undermine the new nation and discourage them from competing.

The "Balance of Payments Reports" was one of the 215 Federal Law Reports I sold for law publisher Commerce Clearing House, CCH. From WWII to the Reagan presidency, America was a net exporter of manufactured goods to the world. In the 1980's we passed the tipping point and imported more than we exported.

The Office of the United States Trade Representative (USTR) recommends United States trade policy to the president. They claim, "Every $1 billion of exports of American goods supports more than 6,000 additional jobs here at home. And every billion dollars of services exports is estimated to support more than 4,500 jobs."

Have they ever looked at the other side of that coin? If $1 billion in exports supports 10,500 US jobs, then is very $1 billion in IMPORTS destroying 10,500 tax paying jobs in America?

We can only wish our Trade Deficit were a paltry $1 billion. The Commerce Department reported our Trade Deficit in just the October-December quarter of 2011 was $124.1 billion. (Associated Press, March 24, 2012.) Do the math. Is that 10,500 lost jobs times 124, or 1,302,000 jobs lost?

Ending FREE TRADE will bring back thousands of good jobs. Those American jobs will pay taxes, cut debt and support families.

Should Congress end FREE TRADE and ban imports of things we can build ourselves? The tax paying jobs will strengthen our nation and provide good jobs for working Middle Class families.

End of chapter

Chapter 25

FAIR AND EQUAL TRADE

What if America ends FREE TRADE and demands FAIR AND EQUAL TRADE instead? We could only import as much as we export. That would end trade deficits in manufactured goods.

Most Americans now know that almost anything they pick up in any store has a 50% chance of being 'Made in China.' Sadly, China buys little from America and has gained a huge trade advantage.

China is the most populous nation on planet Earth. Their 1.35 billion people are more than four times America's population. China's "one child per family" policy to limit population growth has produced a surplus of males their Communist leaders would be able to sacrifice in nationalistic wars.

One of their present goals is developing a navy capable of challenging U.S. Dominance of the oceans. To that end, the pennies of profit derived from every purchase of a Chinese product by an American consumer may come back to us as rockets.

China announced in October 2013 that they have a fleet of nuclear submarines patrolling the world's oceans. It has also been reported that China is developing rockets capable of sinking U. S. Aircraft Carriers. Consider the pain they could inflict in a Pearl Harbor or 911 type sneak attack.

Pearl Harbor left 2,402 dead.
911 left 2,996 dead.
Nuclear attacks on three aircraft carries could kill over 19,000.

Should we continue to allow China a trade advantage?

Should we elect persons who borrowed billions from China?

Should Wall Street be allowed to finance Chinese enterprises?

End of chapter

Chapter 26

THE ENEMY WITHIN

President John F. Kennedy and his brother Robert were both murdered by American citizens. The Federal Building in Oklahoma City was blown up by an American citizen. Horrific as those events were, there is a far greater threat that the media is quiet about.

In 1966 Democrats controlled the presidency and both houses of Congress. Two Columbia University professors and political activists Richard Cloward (1926–2001) and Frances Fox Piven (b. 1932), launched a plan to a bankrupt America by overloading our social services.

Their goal was changing America to suit their vision of a world where the poor would not have to work for a living. They wanted a guaranteed annual wage without work requirements.

The married pair focused on forcing the Democratic Party to take federal action to help the poor. But first, they needed control of the Democratic Party. They planned to employ Community Organizers to ferment unrest and produce "Change."

Are they destroying the America of the Founding Fathers?

Are they destroying the America millions of our citizens died for?

I urge every American to educate themselves to this subversive threat by Goggling "Cloward-Piven Strategy."

End of chapter

Chapter 27

What is a Community Organizer?

Here are President Obama's own words of what he planned to do as a Community Organizer.

The following was published in the National Review Online of October 30, 2013, under the byline of Byron York.

"Even Obama didn't know when he first gave it a try back in 1985. "When classmates in college asked me just what it was that a community organizer did, I couldn't answer them directly," Obama wrote in his memoir, Dreams from My Father. "Instead, I'd pronounce on the need for change. Change in the White House, where Reagan and his minions were carrying on their dirty deeds. Change in the Congress, compliant and corrupt. Change in the mood of the country, manic and self-absorbed. Change won't come from the top, I would say. Change will come from a mobilized grass roots."

Now step back in time, from 2013 to 2006. The debate was about President Bush raising the National debt limit to $9 trillion. Mr. Obama, then a freshman Senator from Illinois, published the following statement in the Congressional Record.

"Increasing America's debt weakens us domestically and internationally. Leadership means that "the buck stops here." Instead, Washington is shifting the burden of bad choices today onto the backs of our children and grandchildren.

"America has a debt problem and a failure of leadership. Americans deserve better.

"I therefore intend to oppose the effort to increase America's debt limit."

Barack Obama
March 16, 2006

End of chapter

Chapter 28

Here is the "Change"

Just as he promised in 1985, President Barack Obama has produced "Change."

From 2006 to 2016 the National Debt has more than doubled from $9 trillion to over $18.5 trillion, mostly under President Obama. The credit rating of America has been downgraded, which will raise future borrowing costs again. On October 1, 2013, the Government was shut down in a budget fight.

One way to look at the two party system is to view it as a marriage. Two spouses have different views on responsibility to live within their means. To those outside of Washington, it sometimes looks like a Hatfield married a McCoy.

The Democratic Party controlled the Senate, but they had failed to pass a budget in four years. Despite their failure, in Oct. 2013 they wanted Republicans to approve another massive spending bill for Obamacare.

By 2016 President Obama will seek to raise the nations debt limit to more than double the $9 billion he opposed in 2006 when he accused President Bush of a "Failure of Leadership."

If raising the debt limit to $9 trillion under President Bush was a Failure of Leadership as defined by then Senator Obama, what can we label President Obama's actions when he forces the nation to raise the debt ceiling limit above $18.5 trillion?

The US Dollar is the "Reserve Currency" of the world. The debts run up by Democrats threaten that status. If we lose that ranking due to a world wide loss of confidence in our nations money , every American will suffer for decades, and perhaps generations.

Would it be reasonable to say that America needs new leadership? Jefferson and Franklin would shout "YES! Yes!"

End of chapter

Chapter 29

WERE WE WARNED OF THIS DANGER?

"Freedom is never more than one generation away from extinction; it's not something we pass along in our bloodstream.
Ronald Reagan

"We the People are the Rightful Masters of both Congress & the Courts, not to Overthrow the Constitution, but Overthrow the men who pervert the Constitution."
Abraham Lincoln

"A private central bank issuing the public currency is a greater menace to the liberties of the people than a standing army...We must not let our rulers load us with perpetual debt." ~Thomas Jefferson

Are thoughts like those above newly minted since the birth of Christianity?

History answered that question perfectly.

"The budget must be balanced, the treasury must be refilled, public debt must be reduced, the arrogance of officaldom must be tempered & controlled, and assistance to foreign lands must be curtailed lest Rome become bankrupt.

"People must again learn to work, instead of living on public assistance."

Cicero, in the Roman Senate, 55 BC

End of chapter

Chapter 30

DOES HISTORY WARN OF OTHER DANGERS?

Alexander Tytler, (15 October 1747 – 5 January 1813) was a Scottish advocate, judge, writer and historian who served as Professor of Universal History, and Greek and Roman Antiquities, in the University of Edinburgh. He wrote this about democracy.

"A democracy is always temporary in nature; it simply cannot exist as a permanent form of government. A democracy will continue to exist up until the time that voters discover that they can vote themselves generous gifts from the public treasury. From that moment on, the majority always votes for the candidates who promise the most benefits from the public treasury, with the result that every democracy will finally collapse due to loose fiscal policy, which is always followed by a dictatorship. The average age of the world's greatest civilizations from the beginning of history has been about 200 years. During those 200 years, these nations always progressed through the following sequence:

Step 1.   From bondage to spiritual faith;
Step 2.   From spiritual faith to great courage;
Step 3.   From courage to liberty;
Step 4.   From liberty to abundance;
Step 5.   From abundance to selfishness;
Step 6.   From selfishness to complacency;
Step 7.   From complacency to apathy;
Step 8.   From apathy to dependence;
Step 9.   From dependence back into bondage."

If America is to survive another 10 years, we must take heed of Cicero's warning of 55 B.C. "People must again learn to work, instead of living on public assistance."

And Captain John Smith: "Those that will not work will not eat."

End of chapter

Chapter 31

CAN AMERICA SURVIVE DEMOCRACY

Can modern Democrats answer the call of John F. Kennedy?

"Ask not what your country can do for you.
Ask instead what you can do for your country."

Do Americans know their History?

Most school children learned about the Declaration of Independence and the Forth of July in 1776. More facts: The first shots were fired on April 19, 1775 in the Battle of Lexington and Concord, near Boston, Massachusetts.

The war lasted 8 years, 4 ½ months, to September 3, 1783.

Four years later the 13 Colonies set about writing a new set of laws to guide the new nation. At the conclusion of the Constitutional Convention in 1787 the delegates left the building. A Mrs. Powel of Philadelphia asked Benjamin Franklin, "Well, Doctor, what have we got?"

With no hesitation, Franklin replied, "A republic, if you can keep it." Not a democracy, not a democratic republic. But "a republic, if you can keep it."

A wise man, he would have known of the fall of the Roman Empire. He could have been sharing his knowledge by way of a warning to the first citizens of a new republic to be careful not to forfeit what so much blood and pain had bought.

If Benjamin Franklin were alive today, he would quote the prior page. He would then declare that our Republic is on step 7 or 8. Wise old Ben would then weep because the Congress has ignored his warning. Democrats are now pushing us toward America's predicted end and many working families back into bondage.

End of chapter

Chapter 32

SHOULD PENSION FUNDS UNDERMINE AMERICA?

Pension and mutual fund managers are all driven by the profit motive. A single down quarter can cost highly compensated and skilled persons their jobs. Despite that risk, should there be limits on where non-taxed monies are invested?

I must reveal my two roles in creating this problem.

First: In 1972 I appeared before the House Ways and Means Committee in Washington and proposed the Two Earner Tax Deduction. I stated that when a spouse went to work leaving the children in the care of others he or she incurred extra expenses. I argued that such expenses should be considered 'Expenses in Production of Income' and therefore tax deductible.

Ways and Means Chairman Wilbur Mills requested I meet privately with him outside the hearing room. I said to him:
"I see some unfairness in the tax laws. I see how big executives can salt away tens of thousands of dollars a year in corporate pension plans, and get a double tax break. The corporation gets a tax deduction, and the executives don't have to pay tax on the money the corporation put into their pension.
"That's good for the big shots. But the little people are left out. The people who work for small businesses have no pension plans. Every dollar they earn is taxed. When they try to save for retirement, or to buy a house, the interest they earn on savings is taxed at their highest rate on top of their salary.
"Mr. Chairman, can you do something to help the average working family save for retirement in some kind of a tax sheltered way?"

He moved swiftly. On Labor Day 1974 President Gerald R. Ford created the Individual Retirement Accounts, IRAs, under ERISA.

Forty two years of savings later, IRAs total $7.6 trillion.

End of chapter

Chapter 33

MY SECOND ROLE

About five years after my conversation with Chairman Mills I received a print-out of my investments in the generous corporate profit sharing plan of my then employer, CCH. I wrote the following letter to the President of the corporation.

Dear Mr. Bartlett,

I just received my annual report reflecting the status of my investment in the company's profit sharing plan.

First, I'd like to thank you and the management for having a profit sharing plan. Second, I'd like to point out that for every dollar the Company and I have invested in the plan over the past five years, together with five years of compound interest, every dollar is now worth only ninety-five cents.

Isn't there a better way?

The next day my boss called me into his office and closed the door. Moments later he took the stance of a dominant guerilla. He leaned forward on his right thumb and shouted. "If I had a button to push and drop you 15 floors into the basement, I'd be pushing it right now!"

A week later, Bob Bartlett, President of Commerce Clearing House, flew from Chicago to New York. He was walking towards me with his hand outstretched.

"Jim," he said, "that was a wonderful letter you wrote me, and I thank you for it. I know how to be the president of this great company, but I don't know how to manage money. However, I'm changing the way the profit sharing plan is managed. I'm bringing in professional money managers and creating choices so that you and every other employee can have greater control over how your pension money is invested."

CCH is the best-known publisher of Pension Plan Law. True to his word, Mr. Bartlett linked up top shelf money managers. Word spread person-to-person, company-to-company, and corporation-to-corporation. I didn't know how or where it linked, but pretty soon Congress created 401k and similar plans. In about one decade everyone with a pension had new rights.

End of chapter

Chapter 34

CAN PENSION FUNDS WORK AGAINST AMERICA?

Americans hate limits. But we need some.

Fund managers are driven to maximize return on investment. Are some pension funds being invested in companies competing with the firms that funded the pensions?

Should American pension funds invest in foreign firms? Should funds invest pensions overseas that work against the best interest of the workers whose cash is in the pension fund?

Should America allow that? Should companies allow that? Should Unions allow that?

During the American Revolution Benjamin Franklin traveled to France seeking financial support. Our founding Fathers knew that Capital was a Weapon of War. Our leaders should know that too.

I propose that all tax favored funds, Pensions, IRA's, 401k's etc., be invested 100% in the United States of America.

Individuals investing their own money should be allowed to go offshore as long as their funds are not and never were tax favored nor backed by our government or any American insurance company.

Should there be a limit on those people? If they are using personal homes as sources of investment funds, and taking tax deductions for mortgages on their homes, should they lose the mortgage deduction by investing off shore? Franklin would say Yes!

America clearly needs to review the entire tax code to end all taxpayer support beyond the basic tax deduction to aid families own at least one personal home.

Families are the key to nationhood.

End of chapter

Chapter 35

The following is from my 1988 book, AFTER BLACK MONDAY

"I now propose that the IRA program be expanded and renamed the Family Wealth Builder Account or FWBA. This proposal is rooted in the knowledge capital formation is vital to American Capitalism, and that millions of younger families did not participate in IRA's because they had more pressing needs.

"The FWBA concept recognizes that Americans have a chronic problem with not saving enough, and a tax incentive may improve this record. The FWBA also recognizes that a married couple should share ownership equally, even if only one of them works for wages.
The one who stays home also works, sometimes harder than the one who gets paid.

"In our conception, FWBA funds would be allowed to be interchanged or converted tax free from one type of asset to another many times, so long as the assets were in the nature of long term saving. As a lifetime tool, the FWBA would allow young families to save for a first house tax free.

"Upon the sale of a home, the proceeds could be 'parked' in a FWBA account for several years if necessary for any reason, then taken out and invested into another home.

"We believe the Family Wealth Builder Accounts could fill an important national role in capital formation, while helping millions of families work their way up the ladder of personal financial security."

By encouraging every family to create savings accounts as prerequisites to home ownership, we will rein in inflation. Home loans would come from Savings and Loans Associations, without causing the inflation that commercial bank loans cause.

That will also cut the national debt by reducing the grand total value of home mortgage tax deductions.

End of chapter

Chapter 36

WE <u>CAN</u> PAY OFF OUR NATIONAL DEBT

President Truman set up a three way borrowing tug-of-war among government, business, and families. The government subsidizes it's competitors. The highest tax brackets get the most help.

President Reagan established a Debt Reduction Committee in the 1980's. Other Presidents have done the same. They all failed.

None of them fully understood that it is the Truman-tug-of-war that is driving America deeper in debt.

This proposed EQUITY PREFERENCE TAX CODE will end that self-defeating tug-of-war. It will eliminate all tax deductions for interest on borrowed money, except for home ownership. Even that may need limits to assure fairness to all citizens.

Predictable benefits of an EQUITY PREFERENCE TAX CODE.

The U.S. Treasury will be able to refinance the National Debt at progressively lower interest rates over time.

Every business will reduce debt via lower interest rates.

Every governmental unit will enjoy lower borrowing costs.

Every educational institution will have lower borrowing costs.

Every church will praise lower borrowing costs.

Every mortgaged family will celebrate lower borrowing costs.

Every student loan debtor will profit by lower borrowing costs.

Every nation will gain strength from lower borrowing costs.

End of chapter

Chapter 37

LIMIT INDIVIDUAL BORROWING

The following was downloaded from a Government web site.

"The Federal Reserve System, often referred to as the Federal Reserve or simply "the Fed," is the central bank of the United States. It was created by the Congress to provide the nation with a safer, more flexible, and more stable monetary and financial system. The Federal Reserve was created on December 23, 1913, when President Woodrow Wilson signed the Federal Reserve Act into law. Today, the Federal Reserve's responsibilities fall into four general Areas.

"Conducting the nation's monetary policy by influencing money and credit conditions in the economy in pursuit of full employment and stable prices.

"Supervising and regulating banks and other important financial institutions to ensure the safety and soundness of the nation's banking and financial system and to protect the credit rights of consumers.

"Maintaining the stability of the financial system and containing systemic risk that may arise in financial markets.

"Providing certain financial services to the U.S. government, U.S. financial institutions, and foreign official institutions, and playing a major role in operating and overseeing the nation's payments Systems."

End of download

The Fed was created in response to the banking panic of 1907. Speculators were trying to 'corner the market' in a company with borrowed money. The deal fell apart, causing a run on banks. The third largest bank in NY collapsed.

The nation was saved when Mr. J. P. Morgan pledged his personal fortune to secure the banks and help America.

Observation: The recent housing crash was caused by people and companies engaging in excessive leveraged borrowing. Again!

End of chapter

Chapter 38

REVIEWING THINGS PAST

The earliest speculative market crash involved the Dutch Tulip Golden Age in March 1637. At the peak of tulip mania, some single tulip bulbs sold for more than 10 times the annual income of a skilled craftsman. The term "tulip mania" is now often used metaphorically to refer to any large economic bubble when asset prices deviate from their true underlying values.

It can be concluded that people eager for easy profit put themselves in debt in hope of making bigger profits in a short time.

In 1929, millions of ordinary folks began speculating. They bought shares on the NY Stock Exchange with 20% cash, 80% on margin. The theory was that using margin would yield five times greater profit.

That same reasoning is now fueled with the added incentive of a tax deduction for interest on borrowed money and low taxes on capital gains. The weak hands in the market are forced out on dips.

Many investor use borrowed funds, made attractive by low rates set by the FED. When the FED raised interest rates, markets turned against the investors. With a need for cash, they sold shares, and the price dropped. Every time the price dropped, more people hit their preset "SELL" points. Computer programs triggered free fall.

That is how many innocent people got hurt when the Dow Jones Industrial Average dropped 22.6%, on October 19, 1987, BLACK MONDAY. Ditto the Dot Com and housing bubbles. (One due?)

Compare that to a horse racing track. The gambler bets $100. Horse loses. Game over. The only one hurt is the one who placed a bad bet. Eliminate margin buying and the only one who can be hurt is the buyer. No one else needs to suffer.

Should all stock investors put up 'cash on the barrel head' as required in the beginning under the Buttonwood tree where stock trading began on Wall Street in 1792?

End of chapter

Chapter 39

DIGESTING A NEW CONCEPT

TAX THE RICH policies initiated by President Truman have made it very difficult for young married couples. Many wanting to start families find it near impossible to buy homes. Low interest rates launched the Baby Boom. We need to bring back pre-Korean War (1947-1949) mortgage loan rates.

Builders are reluctant to build 'starter' homes like those that launched the Baby Boom due to small profit margins.

Untold numbers of unwed mothers get housing paid for by the taxpayers, unfairly burdening married couples with higher taxes.

Several presidents have appointed committees to overhaul the tax code, but they all failed for the same simple reason.

They are trapped in the mindset that interest on borrowed money is a tax deduction for a business. It is time to break that mold.

Look again at the CPI graph in Chapter 8. The unlimited tax deduction for interest on borrowed money is the driving force behind runaway inflation.

Look again the National Debt graph in Chapter 9. That same deduction is the driving force behind our unsustainable National Debt.

Look again at the growing Trade Deficit graph in Chapter 10. High taxes are the driving force behind outsourcing that is growing our trade deficit. Our Trade Deficit is the driving force behind high unemployment and resulting homelessness.

Young voters must tell Congress what they are doing is not working, and an Equity Preference Tax Code will correct many seemingly intractable problems!

End of chapter

Chapter 40

FOUR MORTGAGE RATES
Comparing interest cost as % of loan
All based on the same $100,000 loan.
(All of these rates have applied since WWII ended in 1945)

Comparing interest cost for different rates and years

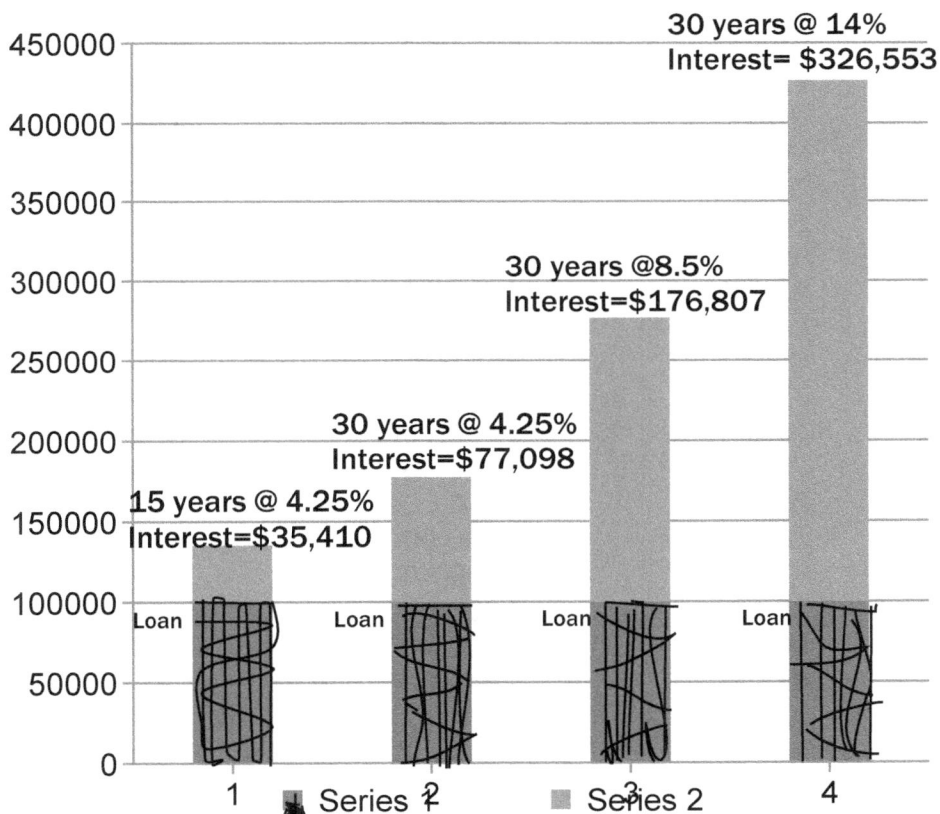

Young married couples must compete with insurance companies, hedge funds, tax shelters, billionaires, the U.S. and foreign governments to borrow money to buy a home. Unmarried mothers get taxpayer supported housing, adding additional burdens on young married families.

An Equity Preference Tax Code would help correct this injustice.

End of chapter

41

Chapter 41

TAX RATES 1963
President Kennedy's 3rd year in office

Tax Rate	Over	But Not Over
20.0%	$0	$4,000
22.0%	$4,000	$8,000
26.0%	$8,000	$12,000
30.0%	$12,000	$16,000
34.0%	$16,000	$20,000
38.0%	$20,000	$24,000
43.0%	$24,000	$28,000
47.0%	$28,000	$32,000
50.0%	$32,000	$36,000
53.0%	$36,000	$40,000
56.0%	$40,000	$44,000
59.0%	$44,000	$52,000
62.0%	$52,000	$64,000
65.0%	$64,000	$76,000
69.0%	$76,000	$88,000
72.0%	$88,000	$100,000
75.0%	$100,000	$120,000
78.0%	$120,000	$140,000
81.0%	$140,000	$160,000
84.0%	$160,000	$180,000
87.0%	$180,000	$200,000
89.0%	$200,000	$300,000
90.0%	$300,000	$400,000
91.0%	$400,000 and over	

KEY FACT: Tax rates had 24 brackets in 1963 under J. F. Kennedy. That provided a gradual increase in the rate for all income groups.

Note 1: At the $50,000 income level the marginal rate went from 69% under FDR to 72% under Truman to 59% under Kennedy .

Note 2: The 91% rate went from "over $200,000" under Truman to "over $400,000" under Kennedy .

End of chapter

Chapter 42

TAX RATES 1987
President Reagan's 2nd term

	Married Filing Jointly	
Marginal		Tax Brackets
Tax Rate	Over	But Not Over
15.0%	$0	$29,750
28.0%	$29,750 -	

This is not a printing error. President Reagan cut the number of brackets from 24 under FDR, Truman, and Kennedy to just two.

The 28% top rate replaced the earlier 91% under Truman and Roosevelt, and 70% top rate under Kennedy.

President Reagan coined the phrase, "structural deficit" as he tried to balance the budget and reduce the national debt.

His "structural deficit" announcement indicated Reagan was aware there was some interactive mathematics in the tax code, but he could never quite give it a definitive label, explanation or solution.

Question: Would Ronald Reagan have appreciated my discovery of why high income tax rates are counterproductive?

Might he have adopted this Equity Preference Tax code?

What prize might he have bestowed?

End of chapter

Chapter 43

TAX RATES 2013
President Obama's 2nd term

Marginal Tax Rate	Married Filing Jointly Tax Brackets	
	Over	But Not Over
10.0%	$0	$17,850
15.0%	$17,850	$72,500
25.0%	$72,500	$146,400
28.0%	$146,400	$223,050
33.0%	$223,050	$398,350
35.0%	$398,350	$450,000
39.6%	$450,000	

Observation: The 39.6% personal income tax rate still makes it very beneficial for high income persons to use leverage, which in turn raises the cost of borrowing for all, from the U.S. Treasury to each and every person on Planet Earth.

In the second term of the Obama administration, many post college age people are back to living with their parents. This is impacting the American birth rate.

A University of Amsterdam study in 2013 reported a 14 point decline in human intelligence, or IQs. If low birth rates continue among the best educated in the nation, it will undermine the foundation of America, SMART FAMILIES!

An Equity Preference tax code could help America grow a much greater number of useful and productive citizens.

End of chapter

Chapter 44

ENTREPRENEURIAL TAX NEEDS

"Entrepreneurs and their small enterprises are responsible for almost all the economic growth in the United States."
President Ronald Reagan

The founding principle of a TAX CODE is to produce revenue to pay the nation's bills, maintain an excellent credit rating, provide funds for national defense and advocate policies conducive to the raising of families that contribute to the needs of society in peace and at war.

The first English settlement was in Virginia in 1607. The Pilgrims arrived at Plymouth in New England in 1620. There was not a single home, store, office, trading post, or factory when they arrived.

Settlers knew that before anyone could live in a house, they had to build them. They also knew that before anyone could buy a product someone had to make it.

Both settlements organized themselves to meet the needs of families. They worked together to produce food, shelter, warmth and sustainability.

Our tax code needs to encourage that same kind of individual accomplishment, especially domestic self sufficiency.

The first settlers founded America over 400 years ago. Everyone knew they had to work to produce homes, food, and heat to survive.

We salute Captain John Smith for setting the example in 1607 with his wise rule, 'No work, no food.' They did not tolerate free loaders or slackers. I am certain they still fed those too feeble to work.

They demonstrated that "Rights" carried "Responsibilities."

An EQUITY PREFERENCE TAX CODE will deliver many benefits to all Americans much as life was 400 years ago.

End of chapter

Chapter 45

A SMART TAX CODE

The present DEBT PREFERENCE TAX CODE has increased the cost of living for every person on earth. It drove America to the present $18.920,000,000,000 ($18.92 Trillion) National Debt.

The proposed EQUITY PREFERENCE TAX RATE SCHEDULE would look something like this.

	CAPITAL INVESTED	RATE ALLOWED		TAX FREE EARNINGS ALLOWED
First	$25,000	10%	up to	$2,500/year
Next	$50,000	9%	additional	$4,500 "
Next	$75,000	8%	additional	$6,000 "
Next	$100,000	7%	additional	$7,000 "
Next	$100,000	6%	additional	$6,000 "
Next	$150,000	5%	additional	$7,500 "

That would allow $33,500 tax free annually to a small business with $500,000 capital investment. All additional capital: 4% tax free on invested funds. There would be no deduction for borrowed money.

The Treasury Department would set tax rates on higher profits. I would favor up to 20 levels of tax rate brackets from 4% upwards in 1% increments. A top rate of 25% might cover all the needs of Government. When the tax free earnings are considered, the top total effective rate may be less than 20% for most businesses. That will spur investment, create jobs and produce shared prosperity.

Owners could borrow money, but they could not take any tax deduction for interest on those funds. That limit will protect the public interest by preventing high interest loan costs from impacting others.

Decades ago a prior owner of the Empire State Building was deeply in debt, with interest rates over 15%. He got large tax deductions, and the taxpayers paid for much of his debt Interest.

No taxpayer would never be responsible for the debts of any other entity under this proposed EQUITY PREFERENCE TAX CODE.

Chapter 46

A HELPING HAND TAX SHELTER

Congress passed high tax rates for public grandstanding. Then they passed laws that only the rich profit from: Tax Shelters.

The following if from my 1988 book, AFTER BLACK MONDAY.
"Past and present tax shelter laws destroyed manufacturing by making productive investments less attractive than tax shelter investments that received preferential tax write-offs." (Out of print.)

Huge loans were the key, and write-offs added to the National debt. They enrich the rich, hold down working families and increase the National Debt. "Super Star" Helping Hands Tax Shelters could help.

The "Super Star" Tax Shelter plan would give a deduction to high income taxpayers to invest cash only, without debt, in urban renewal or rural housing projects and defer income taxes on the investment. They could also buy existing public housing and sell it to 'current residents only' at a super low interest rate.

This plan will give pride of ownership to the occupants, and replace Section 8 Housing. Sports stars could replace the hated 'Projects.'

They could also invest in new housing to replace blight in cities like Detroit. New jobs will make up the tax loss. Owner occupied buildings experience lower crime rates and help build stronger families.

Future payments from the buyers would produce a lasting cash flow to the "Super Star" beyond their normal peak earnings years.

The athlete, artist or investor would have naming rights to the building or project. They would also gain personal satisfaction in lifting up dozens or hundreds of their fellow Americans.

By giving more people a stronger shot at home ownership, America will cultivate a happy and productive population, cut crime, strengthen families and reduce the national debt. A WIN-WIN-WIN-WIN plan.

End of chapter

Chapter 47

BRING OVERSEAS PROFIT HOME

Many U.S. flag multinational companies have earned large profits overseas. That mountain of capital could be put to work in America building factories, adding jobs, paying taxes, reducing our debt, and strengthening families.

Why isn't it happening?

Because Washington wants to tax those profits again.

Washington is blocking the repatriation of billions of capital, so it helps people in other nations and creates jobs in other nations instead of working for America and Americans!

Observation: That is what my Mom would have called "Cutting off your nose to spite your face."

Let's allow American Multinationals to bring profits home at low tax rates with special conditions. Require, wherever possible, they bring the operations back to America, and train Americans for the jobs.

That will also help reduce the National Debt.

Congress should also find a way to tax offshore call centers at the same rate as call centers on our soil. These are American customers doing business with American firms. Those firms need to be nudged, prodded, taxed, whipped or shamed from the Bully Pulpit of the Oval Office to force companies benefiting from American actions to hire American workers, pay American wages and American taxes.

Every job brought home will lift another American family higher, and help reduce our National Debt.

End of chapter

Chapter 48

IMPLEMENTATION: INSTANT OR GRADUAL?

If Congress adopts an EQUITY PREFERENCE TAX CODE, should it be adopted and enforced overnight? Or phased in over time?

With my earliest business experience having been at Union Carbide International, then their research laboratory, followed by selling law reports as diverse as US Tax and Securities, Aviation, Trade Regulation, British and Australian tax guides, and the even the Papua New Guinea Tax Reports, I suggest gradual adoption.

Specifically, I suggest that for the first four years the tax returns be prepared under both the existing America Tax code, and the new EQUITY PREFERENCE TAX CODE.

The taxes due would be as follows:

Year one:	75% of taxes due under old laws.
	25% of taxes due under new law.
Year two:	50% of taxes due under each set of laws.
Year three:	25% of taxes due under old laws.
	75% of taxes due under new law.
Year four:	100% of taxes due under new law.

While this may sound complicated, it will be 'a piece of cake' for computer programmers in Government and major accounting firms.

While at CCH & COMPUTAX decades ago, one accounting firm produced a 110 pound tax return for several hundred partners off of just one set of input forms.

There are many skilled thinkers in and out of Washington eager to help solve our national mess. In just two years the IRS will know how low to set rates, or they could ask IBM to volunteer "Watson!"

End of chapter

Chapter 49

TOWARD A MORE PERFECT UNION

Congress could add compassion to the tax code.

A. The two-earner tax deduction that I proposed in 1972 was made law by President Reagan. He rescinded it in the Tax Reform Act of 1986.

I read in the New York Times that it was for lack of support from the National Organize of Women. They allegedly opposed a benefit requiring a woman to be married. Sadly, I did not keep that paper.

Considering the large number of unwed mothers getting government handouts, wouldn't it be economically wiser to strength marriage? The children of two-parent families live better their entire lives.

Since families are the backbone of civilization, shouldn't all of our laws provide priority support to couples "married with children?"

B. From time to time a few people get lucky and find a temporary jump in income. They could be winners on game shows like Jeopardy or Wheel of Fortune. Or they could get a big one-time bonus. Or they could be sport or performing arts persons with a spike in income as compared to prior years.

Income Averaging was allowed prior to Reagan's Tax Reform Act of 1986. Inasmuch as an EQUITY BASED TAX CODE will lead the nation out of debt, perhaps Congress could bring that practice back into the Internal Revenue Code. I suggest a 5 year time frame.

This would encourage thousands of entrepreneurs, performing artists, movie makers, athletes and venture capitalists to take risks on new projects as their gain would not be taxed at a one-time high, but be averaged over several years of lower rates.

People who risk their own money create the tax paying jobs.

End of chapter

Chapter 50

INCREASE NATIONAL EFFICIENCY

Webster's Dictionary defines 'efficient' as the ability to do something or produce something without wasting materials, time, or energy: the quality or degree of being efficient (technical).

Eli Whitney's invention of the cotton gin, ('gin' being short for engine) was a giant leap of efficiency. Previously, to sift out a single "point" of cotton lint from its surrounding seeds required ten hard hours of hand labor.

A Union Carbide inventor in Speedway, Indiana, perfected a process of putting tungsten carbide coatings on other metals. It improved Pratt & Whitney, GE and Rolls Royce jet engines and launched commercial jet air travel. I participated as a 'hired inventor.'

My 'efficient' contribution was the recommendation that a new plating plant be set up close to the P&W plant in Connecticut. It 'efficiently' eliminated two 800 mile trips by truck or rail and the double packing and unpacking of delicate compressor blades. In time 24 plants were built around the Free World.

Efficiency can also be applied to save a few minutes a million times daily if America adopts a single standard for the location of data on every invoice or informative form widely used.

Examples: 1. Forms used in the auto industry, phone and utility bills, credit card bills, medical industry and even the cash register receipt from the grocery store require visual searching. Each business now sets their own system. Over 100 million Americans waste time finding data that could have a standardized location.

2. When we bring jobs back to America, mail delivery could be cut to alternate days in the rural 80% of the land, saving billions in fuel and labor. These two suggestions are but the tip of the iceberg.

End of chapter

Chapter 51

GIVE CREDIT WHERE DUE

Rockefeller and the United Nations

The United Nations were established on October 24, 1945. The first office was at Lake Success, Nassau County, New York. I personally walked in those buildings in 1947-1948.

They outgrew the space, and headlines announced that the U.N. was leaving New York.

William Zeckendorf Sr., a real estate developer, though it would hurt America. He telephoned Nelson Rockefeller and told him of a property he owned that would make a suitable home for the World Organization.

Nelson Rockefeller asked his dad to help America and the World at large. John D. Rockefeller Jr. anted up $8.5 million to buy the 17 acre site on the east side of Manhattan as the permanent home for the United Nations.

It was a triumph of American Capitalism and Patriotism.

Whenever American presidents or spokespersons speak at the U.N., or the heads of other nations have the podium, would it be fitting that they acknowledge the contributions of those who made that forum possible?

I never met a Rockefeller family member, but I know they put their oil empire at risk to create jobs in New York City building Rockefeller Center during the Great Depression.

Would it be appropriate if visitors on the UN podium tipped their hat to Rockefeller, Capitalism and American Patriotism?

End of chapter

Chapter 52

GIVE BLAME WHERE DUE
Alan Greenspan's error

All humans make errors. Many only impact the person who made the error. But when the person making the error has great power over the banking system of the world's biggest supper power, unintended disasters can result.

Mr. Greenspan was the 13th Chairman of the U.S. Federal Reserve Bank. His term in office began August 11, 1987. Just two months later he was challenged by the 22% market drop on Black Monday.

His time in office covered the presidencies of Ronald Reagan, George H. W. Bush, Bill Clinton, and George W. Bush.

On his watch we experienced the growth and collapse of the dot.com world. That was followed by the ballooning and inevitable implosion of the housing bubble fiasco.

His term ended January 31, 2006, with America and the world wallowing in a deep recession/depression.

While he served we learned he was a devotee of Ann Rand and the laissez faire or "hands off" style of governing. As Fed chairman, he lived by his conviction that the markets will always correct themselves.

On October 23, 2008, nearly three years after leaving office, he told a Congressional committee, "I was wrong."

I was one of the millions of retirees who saw the value of their savings, pensions, and investments decimated by his mistakes.

The Federal Reserve Board lacks the authority to fix what is wrong with our tax code. The President and Congress must take bold action to save our Republic and the world by adopting an Equity Preference Tax Code.

End of chapter

Chapter 53

WHAT WOULD EINSTEIN SAY?

Imagine, if you will, Congress adopting this proposed EQUITY PREFERENCE TAX CODE. Then try to imagine a future conversation between Dr. Einstein and his tax advisor, Leo Mattersdorf.

"Albert, there is a new Smart Tax law in America to help governments, businesses and families all prosper."

"How will it work, Leo?"

"Business owners will gain some tax free income on capital.

"Banks will still be allowed to lend money.

"Business owners will still be allowed to borrow money.

"But borrowers will not be allowed to shift the cost of their debt to the nation at large, or to other families.

"The beauty of this plan is that it will end investor leverage by the super rich that burdens working middle class families.

"It will end U.S. hidden taxpayer subsidies to the wealthy.

"It will also lower taxes on the wealthy in a fair trade off.

"It will end the lifetime mortgage bondage of many families.

"It will end the need for government backed college loans.

"It will aid America in paying down her $18.5 trillion debt.

"It will allow more funds for schools and education.

"It will take America back to the 1947 world of family building.

"It will allow young couples a bright future to start families.

"It will provide the funds needed to fight all terrorists.

"And most importantly, Albert, it will help America to continue to be a beacon of hope for the world."

Einstein replies, "Now I can finally understand the income tax."

Then Einstein may add, "What I still don't understand is why didn't they use this Smart Tax law years ago?"

Leo replies, "The corporate income tax began in 1912 at 1%. Interest on borrowed money was a tax deduction that became a habit. Apparently, no one questioned the wisdom of doing that for 100 years. Then along came a thinking guy like you, Albert. A simple man who questioned everything."

The End

After words

You have just read some bold and audacious suggestions on how to strengthen America. You can help turn them into future laws.

In 1972 my wife, five children and I journeyed from New York to Washington to ask Congress to help working Middle Class families.

Silent film star Gloria Swanson, allegedly involved with President Kennedy's father, was the lead witness. I was the last and the least.

My family of seven were renting a 700 square foot apartment with gas light fixtures. To get it, we had to decontrol the rent and pay double the former rate. By any standard I was a fool to spend winter coats and shoes money on my wild idea to help others.

In 1972 I proposed the IRA plan to a Ways and Means Chairman who was a Democrat. He shepherded the plan
and secured the signature of a President who was a Republican.

As of June 30, 2016 the Congressional Budget Office reported the total value of all Individual Retirement Accounts at $7.629 Trillion.

As of the date of publication, April 13, 2016, that is many times the value of our most valuable corporations.

Also, if you have sold your home after 1997, you have
benefited
from my effort that led President Clinton to raising the tax-free gain from $125,000 per couple to $500,000 per couple.

There are good and sincere men and woman in Congress that are longing for actions that will achieve national goals. May God lead them to compromise on this Equity Preference Tax code so that millions may gain respectable work and earn wages that support life with dignity.

What will you do to make America better?

James T. Kelly
Middle Class Tax Advocate
and Grandfather of many

GREED BEGAN IN THE WHITE

My closing statement:

In 1950 President Truman took us into his undeclared Korean War. His actions during that war have been silently destroying America like a cancer since 1952.

Shamefully, four people seeking the presidency are clueless regarding this cancer. In a moment I will explain what it is.

But first, a recap of the four politicians seeking the presidency.

Senator Ted Cruz wants to abolish the Internal Revenue Service. He apparently lacks basic knowledge of how our government works. Without the Internal Revenue Service our Government income would be zero!
Senator Cruz is acting childlike, shouting at the wind.
When he calms down, I think he could be a great Attorney General, and a future Justice of the Supreme Court.
Sadly, Senator Cruz is not alone in his lack of tax knowledge.

Hillary Clinton has been living on tax payers' money for 35 years.
Senator Bernie Sanders has been in Congress for 25 years.
Gov. John Kasich was a Congressman for 18 years and ranking member of the House Budget Committee.

Clinton, Cruz, Kasich and Sanders claim they can fix America, but NONE OF THEM UNDERSTAND THAT THE REAL PROBLEM IS THE STRUCTURE OF THE TAX CODE. (Remember President Reagan's words, "Structural Deficit?")

Forgive them. The U.S. Tax Code went counterproductive in 1951 when Sanders was 11, Hillary was in kindergarten and neither Kasich nor Cruz had been born.

A SMART 'Equity Preference' tax code will solve that problem.

James T. Kelly

I am an 87 Year old Korean Vet. This book will help the children and grandchildren of all of our war heroes have more secure lives.   AMEN

www.ingramcontent.com/pod-product-compliance
Lightning Source LLC
Chambersburg PA
CBHW071630170526
45166CB00003B/1274